Just the Facts

Teen
Pregnancy

Mary Nolan

Heinemann Library
Chicago, Illinois

© 2003 Reed Educational & Professional Publishing
Published by Heinemann Library,
an imprint of Reed Educational & Professional Publishing,
Chicago, Illinois

Customer Service 888-454-2279
Visit our website at www.heinemannlibrary.com

Designed by M2 Graphic Design
Illustrations by Catherine Ward, except p.37 by Jeff Edwards.
Originated by Ambassador Litho
Printed in Hong Kong by South China Printers

07 06 05 04 03
10 9 8 7 6 5 4 3 2 1

Library of Congress Cataloging-in-Publication Data
Nolan, Mary, 1956-
  Teen pregnancy / Mary Nolan.
      p. cm. -- (Just the facts)
Includes bibliographical references and index.
Summary: Provides an overview of the issues surrounding teen pregnancy,
including prevention, causes, options, and resources.
  ISBN 1-58810-682-9
 1. Teenage pregnancy--Juvenile literature. 2. Teenage
parents--Juvenile literature. [1. Pregnancy. 2. Teenage parents. 3.
Adoption. 4. Abortion. 5. Contraception.] I. Title. II. Series.
  HQ759.4 .N65 2002
    306.874'3--dc21

                            2001006071

Acknowledgements
The author and publishers are grateful to the following for permission to reproduce copyright material: pp. 5, 7, 13, 33 Corbis; pp. 8, 19 Imagebank; pp. 9, 10, 14, 23, 42, 64 Science Photo Library; pp. 11, 16, 25, 36, 40-41, 45 Bubbles Photo Library; pp. 12, 20 Corbis Stock Market; pp. 15, 34–35 Tudor Photography; pp. 17, 50 Robert Harding Picture Library; pp. 27, 34-35, 38, 49, 51 Stone; p. 43 National Health Service.

Graph on page 6 taken from The Alan Guttmacher Institute web site.

Cover photograph by Wellcome Photo Library.

Every effort has been made to contact copyright holders of any material reproduced in this book. Any omissions will be rectified in subsequent printings if notice is given to the publisher.

Some words are shown in bold, **like this.** You can find out what they mean by looking in the glossary.

Contents

Teen Pregnancy

Every year, thousands of babies are born to teenage parents. Despite a steady decline over the past decade, the teen birth rate in the United States remains the highest among developed countries. According to the National Center for Health Statistics, nearly one million U.S. teenagers became pregnant in 2001. About 5 teenage girls in 100 had a baby.

Too young to be a parent?

Although teenagers can be just as loving as older adults toward babies and children, it can be hard for them, as parents, to give their child emotional and financial security. Some teenagers are in stable relationships. Even so, they are still growing up. Rather than being ready to give attention, they want lots of attention themselves. They have needs of their own which are very hard to put aside in order to respond 24 hours a day to a baby's needs.

A young woman who becomes pregnant may have a more difficult pregnancy than an older woman. She is more likely to have high blood pressure, which can be dangerous both for her and her baby. She is more likely to go into **labor** too early and have a **premature baby** who is underweight. Small babies are more prone to breathing difficulties and are more at risk for **Sudden Infant Death Syndrome** (**SIDS**), sometimes called crib death.

In Western societies, young parents are often given a hard time. They can be accused of being irresponsible, selfish, careless, and immature. The governments of some countries are not prepared to give much help to young mothers, especially if they are unmarried. Politicians often condemn teenage pregnancies. Voters may not like to see their taxes being spent on supporting young parents. This is not to say that there aren't benefits—just that it can be hard to find out what they are and how to claim them. The best people to ask are midwives and social workers, or one of the organizations listed at the end of this book.

For all these reasons, it's hard to be a teenage parent. Many young people who become parents wish they had waited until they were older. It can be difficult to say "no" to sex, but having sex at an early age places young people at risk, not only of pregnancy, but also of **sexually transmitted diseases** and cancer of the **cervix.**

❝It's very easy to get pregnant, but it's very hard to be a parent.❞

(Laura, 17)

Young Parents

In Shakespeare's play, *Romeo and Juliet*, the heroine, Juliet, is about fourteen years old. Yet the other characters in the play seem to think that she is old enough to get married and have a baby. In the past, it was normal for girls to start childbearing at a very early age. Life expectancy was much shorter than it is today. Many babies did not survive infancy, so women had very large families in the hope that a few children would grow to adulthood. For these reasons, it made sense for couples to start their families at a young age. People tended to live in family groups, or small communities, where there was plenty of support for parents and plenty of willing hands to help out with the children. Being young and a mother or father wasn't nearly as difficult as it is today.

Today, people expect to live well into their 70s and beyond. Better sanitation, housing, and health care mean that the majority of babies grow up into healthy children and adults. There's not the same need to start a family early. So why do so many teenage girls become pregnant?

One reason is linked to a lack of confidence. Young women may not feel able to ask their boyfriend to use a **condom.** They don't carry condoms around with them for fear they'll be labeled as "easy."

It won't happen to me

Probably the single most important reason that teenagers get pregnant is that they feel "it will never happen to me." Janine, age 14, explains: "We didn't use a condom. It was my first time. I didn't think you could get pregnant the first time."

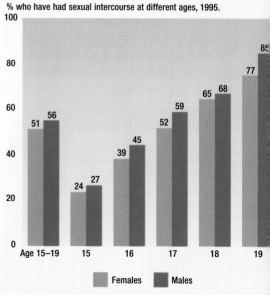

% who have had sexual intercourse at different ages, 1995.

Females   Males

Although this graph shows that only a relatively small percentage of 15 and 16-year-olds are having sex, it doesn't show how often this has resulted in a pregnancy.

Pressures on the young

Media and **peer group** pressures are enormous. Television, magazines, and newspapers are full of stories and pictures about sex, and there's lots of sex talk among teenagers. It's easy for young women and men to feel that perhaps they're the only ones not sleeping with their boyfriend or girlfriend. People might be rushed into sexual relationships before they're really ready.

In fact, figures show that two-thirds of teenagers are still virgins when they reach their sixteenth birthday. About one in five young people do not have **sexual intercourse** until they are in their twenties. Men and women who wait until they are older generally enjoy sex more. It's not necessary to be having sex to have a good social life.

Despite her sexy image, Britney Spears has become a role model for young people who don't believe in having sex before marriage.

Sex and Drugs

The influence of drugs

Drugs are everywhere in today's society. People turn to drugs, whether legal or illegal, as a way of solving their problems. The most widely used, and perhaps the most dangerous of all drugs, is alcohol. Young people (like older people) use alcohol because it helps them relax or makes them feel less depressed (because they meet their friends at a party or club) or because they are the children of parents who abuse alcohol. There is a strong relationship between alcohol abuse and teenage pregnancy.

Other drugs such as cocaine, crack cocaine, marijuana, and stimulants may be used by young people who want to find out what a high is like, or who are part of a group that regularly uses street drugs. The drugs may make them feel temporarily good about themselves, but they also cut them off from reality. Feeling that they can take on the world may lead a person into unsafe sexual behavior.

❝I was stoned. I didn't know where I was or what I was doing. We had sex in the back of the car. The next day I just knew I was pregnant.❞ (Alexis, 15)

Sexual abuse

Pregnancy in very young people is sometimes the result of **abusive relationships** in which a girl is forced to have sex against her will by her father, stepfather, mother's boyfriend, or another male relative. "My stepfather has been abusing me for three years. I got pregnant a while ago and he hit me when I told him. He said I had to have an **abortion** or he'd throw me out." (Lauren, 15).

Some young people come from families where women are dominated by men. For these women, it can be extremely difficult to say "no" if a man asks them to have sex. Sexual abuse saps a young woman's self-esteem. She may react by sleeping around because she feels she's not worth anything anyway.

Organizations that can help young people in abusive relationships are listed at the end of this book.

Taking drugs can lead to unsafe sexual behavior.

9

Baby Challenges

Babies have a wonderful capacity to give love and there are lots of magic moments in the lives of parents with small children. However, being a parent isn't easy. Babies born to very young mothers may have a poorer start in life than the babies of older women. They are more likely to:

- be born too early
- have breathing problems
- have infections during their first years of life
- be at risk of **SIDS.**

During the first months of a baby's life, it's hard to get a good night's sleep. New parents can feel very isolated. Friends who rushed to see the baby when he first came home don't come so often after a while. Mothers have to accept that, for some time, their body is not what it used to be—for example, they may have enlarged breasts, a saggy tummy, and lifeless hair. Fathers have to accept that their partner's attention is now divided between them and the baby.

Young parents also have decisions to make about whether, and how, they are going to continue with their education.

Teenage mothers are more likely to have premature babies.

While governments try to ensure that educational opportunities are available for teenage parents, it can be hard to go back to studying when you have a baby at home.

Girls who get pregnant at an early age often do less well at school, have a higher dropout rate, and have poorer job prospects than their friends whose education wasn't interrupted by a baby.

Some young people say that their baby makes up for the things they have lost: "I spend all my time with my baby. Just having her around is enough for me. I don't envy my friends who've gone to college." (Claire, 16).

Others feel that they are missing out: "If I could go back, I'd definitely wait to get pregnant. There's so much I wanted to do, but I'm tied down by the baby now." (Cherri, 17).

Babies need lots of attention. Even older parents sometimes find it hard to cope.

OK to Be Pregnant?

Some cultures are very accepting of young parents. In these cultures, a girl who has a couple of children by the time she is eighteen is simply doing what her mother and grandmother did before her. She might be part of a supportive, caring community and have friends embarking on motherhood at the same time as herself. She may enjoy mothering her babies and not feel that she has missed out on her youth.

Family support can be very important for all mothers—however young or old they are.

Pregnancy is a time when women receive a lot of attention from a whole range of health and social work professionals. This can provide an opportunity to sort out a drug problem, an **abusive relationship,** or other financial, social, or educational difficulties. It's easier for a girl to ask for help when she knows that the well-being of her baby depends on her. "I'd never had the will power to stop drinking until I got pregnant. The baby made me stop, with a lot of help from my midwife." (Helena, 16).

Pregnancy may draw a young woman back into her family and re-establish a relationship with her parents that was

previously at breaking point. Some families are very good at coming together when there is a crisis to face. However, more families are torn apart by teenage pregnancy than are brought together.

Some young women are thrown out of their homes when they tell their parents they are pregnant. The parents feel ashamed. They are worried about what their relatives and neighbors will say. They may have jobs where it will be difficult for them to admit that their teenage daughter is going to have a baby. They may feel that all their hopes for their daughter's future have been dashed.

Some young women are desperate for love and feel that a baby will love them as they have never been loved before. It is tragic that anyone should feel the need to get pregnant for this reason. It should be remembered that, at least initially, babies take much more love than they give and that small children can be very challenging as well as affectionate.

Pregnancy—Finding Out

Today, pregnancy tests are very accurate. They can tell a woman that she is pregnant very soon after she has conceived a baby. However, there are plenty of natural signs that pregnancy is underway. The most obvious is missing a **period.** Even before this happens, a woman may become aware that her breasts feel very full and tingly, perhaps even painful. Her tummy feels full, although her baby is still tiny. She may feel very tired because her body is busy reorganizing her **circulation** and her digestion to cope with supporting two lives instead of one.

The baby is growing from hour to hour, developing rapidly from a cluster of cells into a recognizable human being. The result of all this frantic activity is that the pregnant woman often feels drained. Some women start to feel sick at the very beginning of pregnancy, and this is the first sign for them that a baby is on the way. Many women say they "just knew" they were pregnant, even before their bodies started telling them.

❝I had a gut feeling I was pregnant.❞

(Maria, 17)

Pregnancy tests

It's helpful for a woman to find out whether she's pregnant as soon as possible. If she is happy to be pregnant, she can start to take special care of herself in order to give her baby the best start in life. If she wants to have an **abortion,** it's safer if the procedure is carried out in the first three months of pregnancy. If she's not sure about the pregnancy, she has time to talk to other people before making any decisions.

Confidential, low-cost (sometimes free) pregnancy tests are available from:

- family planning clinics
- sexual health clinics
- student health centers.

Home pregnancy tests can be obtained from pharmacies, drugstores, or supermarkets.

Pregnancy tests involve mixing a few drops of urine with some chemicals to detect the presence or absence of pregnancy **hormones.** They can be used on the day the woman's period should have started, although they are more reliable if carried out a few days after this.

Home pregnancy tests are easy to use—and give results quickly.

Testing positive

All women feel a strong mixture of emotions when they find out that they're pregnant. They might be shocked, amazed, terrified, excited, and uncertain all at the same time. Girls who are still in school and not in a steady relationship often feel very scared.

Some young women go into a state of denial when they discover they're pregnant. They ignore the early signs of pregnancy and try to pretend that nothing is happening. They may feel that they've let their parents down and be terrified of telling them the news. They may also be frightened of telling their boyfriend. Weeks can pass while they try to decide what to do next. Some girls continue to conceal their pregnancies until the day the baby is due and give birth on their own, or go to the hospital as an emergency.

It's very risky not to get any help. Young women (just like older women) need emotional support to cope with pregnancy and physical care to make

"The pregnancy test said I was pregnant, but I didn't believe it. I was throwing up all the time, but I refused to believe it."

(Leanne, 15)

sure that they remain healthy. Although pregnancy is a healthy experience for most women, things do occasionally go wrong—placing the life of both mother and child in jeopardy.

It's important to talk to someone. Parents are sometimes unexpectedly supportive once they get over the initial shock. "Instead of being angry, my Dad stood there, hugging me…he added that he'd stick by me whatever I did." (Lois, 17).

Other people to talk to are:
- a doctor
- a youth worker
- a school nurse
- a favorite teacher
- an adult friend.

A trusted adult can help the girl break the news to her parents or other important people in her life. "I told my English teacher. She was great. She said I had to tell my parents, but she came with me." (Mylene, 16).

Finding out you're pregnant is easier if there's someone to support you.

Becoming a Father

A young man is likely to be every bit as shocked by the news that his girlfriend is pregnant as she is herself. He may be delighted and feel that he will be more respected by his friends. Or he may be terrified at the thought of how difficult it will be to be a father while he is still at school or in a low-paying job. Some young men are very angry and feel their girlfriend has cheated on them. "She told me she was on the pill and then she got pregnant. She really got me in trouble." (Lewis, 17).

It can be just as hard for a young man to tell his parents that his girlfriend is pregnant as it is for a young woman to tell her parents. He needs as much support as she does to handle the situation. Many boys and young men find it very difficult to express their feelings. Trying to find the right words to talk to their girlfriend may prove impossible. The relationship can come to an end with both partners feeling angry and distressed.

Fathers

Sometimes a boy is contacted months after sleeping with a girl and told that he is the father of her baby. While he may be prepared to shoulder his responsibilities, he still wants to be certain that the baby is his. A **DNA** test after the baby is born may be the only way of solving this problem.

Research shows that the fathers of babies born to teenagers under 16 are, in general, 5 or more years older than the mother. If the teenage girl is under the age of consent (which, depending on the state, ranges from 14 to 18), the father might be frightened of being prosecuted for having sex with an underage girl. Also, the father is required to contribute to the financial upkeep of his child.

There is a list of organizations at the end of this book that offer advice and support to fathers of all ages.

❝I knew my parents would get mad. And they did. And I still had to face my girlfriend's parents.❞

(Mark, 16)

Choosing an Abortion

Sometimes a woman will decide not to continue with her pregnancy. The decision to end a pregnancy is always a difficult one. Even if a girl is quite sure that she doesn't want a baby, an **abortion** is likely to have a profound impact on her. Women who have ended their pregnancies often think for years afterward about the babies they chose not to have. The babies they eventually have do not replace the ones they've lost: They're simply different babies. Any young woman considering an abortion should receive counseling from a qualified nurse, school counselor, or social worker.

It is important to talk things through before deciding on an abortion.

An abortion can be a hazardous procedure if it isn't carried out in a hospital or at a properly registered clinic. Every year, back street abortions lead to serious infections and sometimes death for many women in different parts of the world.

Abortion in the United States is currently legal in all 50 states when performed during the first **trimester** (three months). In a 1973 Supreme Court decision, Roe v. Wade struck down the abortion laws of most states. Under this ruling, no state can regulate abortion during the first trimester of pregnancy.

Current Supreme Court rulings allow the individual states to regulate abortion in various ways, including: banning elective abortions after the first trimester; requiring parental consent or notice before a minor can obtain an abortion; requiring waiting periods before an abortion may be performed (usually 24-48 hours); and, requiring informed consent or counseling be obtained before an abortion.

Early abortions

If the pregnancy is less than eight weeks, it can be terminated by using an abortion pill and gel which is put into the vagina to make the **womb** contract and expel the **fetus.**

The so-called abortion pill—the drug RU-486 (Mifepristone)—is actually a series of pills that cause an abortion very early in pregnancy. RU-486 is widely used in Europe, and was approved for use in the United States in 2000. A woman must see her doctor to get a prescription for RU-486.

Having a sympathetic person to talk to in the days after the abortion is very important. "I was so relieved when I woke up after the operation. I felt great—everything was going to be OK. I could get on with my life. But a couple of days later, it really hit me what I'd done. And I was very sad for a long while after that, thinking about my baby." (Carla, 14).

Late abortion

There are two ways of ending a pregnancy that has progressed beyond the first **trimester.** A medical **abortion** is when drugs are used to make the woman's body go into **labor** and push the baby out of the **womb.** Going into labor when there's not going to be a living baby at the end is a traumatic experience. Once the womb starts to contract, the abortion can be very painful, and doctors generally prescribe strong pain-relieving drugs to keep the woman comfortable.

In some hospitals, late abortions are carried out as a surgical procedure. The neck of the womb is stretched open and the baby is removed surgically. The thought of this is very distressing to some women, and they prefer to go to a hospital or clinic that offers medical abortion.

The abortion procedure become more difficult and distressing the longer the pregnancy progresses.

Molly's story

"I was fifteen when I got pregnant and I was living with foster parents. I knew right away that I couldn't keep the baby, but I was four months along before I told my social worker. She felt I was right to have an abortion and she said there was no need to tell my parents because I'd had a lot of trouble with my dad in the past and my mom always supported him. The abortion took about ten hours, but I didn't have any pain because of all the drugs they gave me. I saw the baby when it was born—just quickly. I think I made the right decision to have the abortion, but next time I get pregnant, it has to be for keeps."

Adoption and Foster Care

Some young women do not agree with **abortion,** or they feel that they could not put themselves through the stress of terminating their pregnancy. However, they know that they don't have the emotional or financial resources to cope with a baby. For them, adoption is a possibility.

Adoption is a big decision. The mother will need counseling and the support of a social worker to help her think through the pros and cons very carefully. Once the adoption has gone through the courts, she will no longer be the legal parent of her child. In all states, the birth mother and birth father hold the "right of consent" to adoption of their child.

Difficult decisions

It's impossible to make a definite decision about adoption until after the baby is born. Pregnancy is a time of tumultuous feelings; birth is a major life event. Only after the birth can a mother be really sure of her feelings. A girl considering adoption can see her baby after she has given birth. She can hold him and spend some time with him. It seems to be easier to cope with the grief of giving up a baby if the mother has a picture in her mind of the person for whom she is grieving.

Occasionally, those who adopt allow the birth mother to continue to see her baby. Others are prepared to send an annual report with photographs of the child, but do not want any face-to-face contact. Some birth mothers do not wish to see their child again, preferring a clean break.

Foster care is an alternative to adoption. A member of the birth mother's own family might care for the baby until the mother is ready to look after him herself. She remains the legal parent.

Birth parents can sometimes keep in touch with their adopted children. Sometimes they receive photographs or other momentos or reminders of their child.

CHECKED BY

Temp
Vitamin K give

Keeping the Baby

Many young women have strong views about **abortion,** but would find it too difficult to give up their baby for adoption. So they decide to keep their baby. This isn't an easy decision, and there are a number of factors that are likely to influence its success.

First, the mother needs support during pregnancy and after the birth, preferably from adults with an understanding of what life is like with a young child. Some young fathers are prepared to support their partners emotionally, even if they are unable to make a financial contribution. Often, however, relationships break up during the young woman's pregnancy or shortly after the birth of the baby: "I wasn't ready for fatherhood. I couldn't cope with being tied down, and my girlfriend changed when she had the baby. She didn't want me as much." (Josh, 17).

Financial security

Financial security is essential. If the mother's family can't help her, she needs to apply for welfare benefits. Benefits can be complicated, especially for young people. Social workers and counselors can help with the various forms.

Most importantly, the young mother needs to consider how having a baby will affect her life over the next few years. She needs to think about whether she will continue her education, where she can find help with the baby, and how she can improve her job prospects. There are numerous expenses, such as clothes, diapers, and a crib, car seat, and stroller.

There's a lot to think about at a time when the girl's body is going through tremendous changes and confused emotions. This is why having someone to talk to whom she trusts and respects is so important.

"I don't think I could have managed without my mom. She was great—kept me sane, really."

(Adrianna, 17)

Being Pregnant

A normal pregnancy can last from 37 to 42 weeks. To find out when the baby might be due, the doctor adds nine months and seven days to the date on which the girl's last period started. For example:

First day of last period	Baby due
January 14th	October 21st
June 7th	March 14th
September 3rd	June 10th

This is called the Estimated Date of Delivery or Expected Date of Delivery (EDD), but it is only an estimation, a rough guide to when the baby might be born.

Doctors and midwives divide pregnancy into three sections, called **trimesters.** Each trimester covers three months. In the first trimester, pregnant women tend to be tired and rather unpredictable—happy one minute and depressed the next. The woman's body is being totally reorganized to look after her unborn baby.

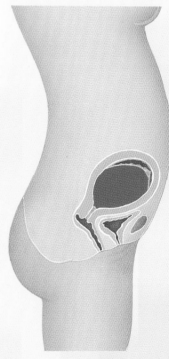

The pregnancy is just beginning to show.

16 weeks

During the second trimester, the pregnant woman generally feels much more positive. Her energy levels pick up and, at about twenty weeks, she can finally start to feel her baby making tiny fluttering movements inside her.

Her tummy starts to swell and other people notice that she's pregnant.

By 26 weeks, the baby is moving quite vigorously and the top of her bump is above her belly button.

In the third trimester, the weight of the baby can make being pregnant very uncomfortable. Backaches, swollen ankles, and aching legs are common as the woman's heavy belly gets in the way of the circulation to her legs. Finding a comfortable sleeping position isn't easy. Sleep can be further disturbed by the need to go to the bathroom frequently because the baby is pressing down on the **bladder.** As the mother's EDD approaches, she can start to feel very apprehensive about the labor, as well as excited at the prospect of seeing her baby. "By nine months, I was fed up with being pregnant. I just wanted to see the baby." (Kim, 15).

Maternity clothes are definitely needed now.

28 weeks

Being so large is exhausting.

36 weeks

The baby inside

The first three months of pregnancy are when the baby is growing most rapidly. As early as six weeks after conception, its heart can be seen beating on an **ultrasound scan.** By twelve weeks, his or her kidneys are fully functional and are making urine. Blood is circulating around the body; the baby can suck and swallow and it is possible to detect his or her sex organs.

From twelve to twenty weeks, the baby's skeleton takes shape. The nose forms and the two parts of the palate of the mouth join together. The skin becomes covered with soft downy hair called **lanugo.** Fingernails start to grow. The baby moves more and more vigorously and, by twenty weeks, the mother can feel him or her wriggling inside her.

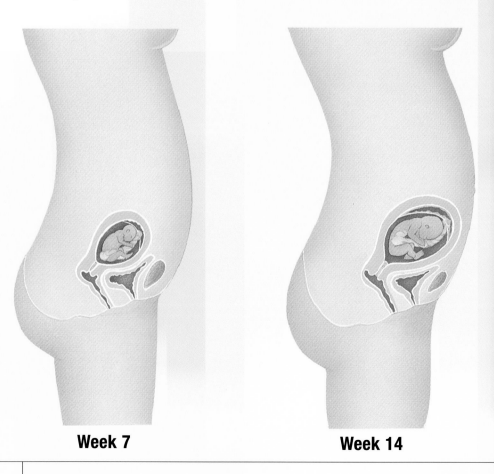

Week 7   **Week 14**

Halfway through

Halfway through the pregnancy, the baby starts to develop a pattern of sleeping and waking which the mother quickly learns to recognize. The baby can now hear and distinguish between different sounds. By the time he is born, the baby is able to recognize his mother's voice. If he were to be born at 24 weeks of pregnancy, there would be a small chance of survival. Chances of survival increase with every additional week spent inside the **womb.**

By 28 weeks, the baby's eyelids are open and he or she can distinguish between light and dark. The baby is making shallow breathing movements, getting lungs ready for birth. In the final twelve weeks of pregnancy, the baby's skin, which has been red and wrinkled, becomes smooth. Most of the hair that has covered the body disappears. Stores of fat are laid down which make the face and body rounded.

The fat will provide the baby with energy for birth and for the first few days of life when the mother has only small amounts of breast milk to give. The hair on the head and the nails grow rapidly and the bones of the skull become harder.

By the end of pregnancy, nature has carefully prepared the baby for life outside the womb. Unlike most other mammals, however, the child will be highly dependent on its mother for years to come.

Week 30

Toward the end of pregnancy, most babies settle into a head-down position.

Pregnancy Lifestyle

Pregnant women share their lives with their unborn babies in a very intimate way. Whatever they eat and drink, their babies must also eat and drink; if they smoke, their babies have to smoke; if they catch an infection, their babies run the risk of catching it as well. So it's very important for an expectant mother to take care of herself and give her baby a good start in life.

Folic acid

Research has shown that babies are less likely to develop **spina bifida**—a deformity that can cause paralysis—if the mother takes extra folic acid while she is pregnant. Although folic acid is present in foods such as dark green leafy vegetables, and is often added to flour, bread, and cereals, it's still wise to take a supplement. Supplements can be purchased at a pharmacy.

Infections

Infections such as **rubella** and chicken pox can damage the unborn baby. Pregnant women should also avoid children who are ill, or who have recently been **vaccinated.**

Another source of infection is cat litter, which may contain an organism called *Toxoplasma gondii*, which causes **toxoplasmosis** in humans. Pregnant women should always wear gloves to empty a litter box or when gardening, as soil may be contaminated with cat feces.

Diet

The usual rules of a good diet apply during pregnancy—plenty of fresh fruits and vegetables and plenty of carbohydrates such as bread, pasta, and potatoes. Protein is required in moderation in the form of meat and eggs. Vitamins are also important, but should be taken only on the advice of a doctor; too much of certain vitamins can harm the baby. Sweet sugary foods should be kept for special treats—they're not an essential part of a good diet.

There are a few foods to avoid, also. These include liver, soft cheeses such as brie and camembert, blue-veined cheeses, paté, uncooked meats, and raw or lightly boiled eggs. All of these foods may contain harmful bacteria.

It's important to have a very healthy diet during pregnancy, with plenty of fresh fruits and vegetables.

Drugs and Pregnancy

Many women find it possible to kick problem habits during pregnancy. There are lots of organizations that will help pregnant girls deal with drug, alcohol, tobacco, or substance abuse. Some are listed at the end of this book.

Experts disagree on how much alcohol is safe to drink during pregnancy, but everyone is certain that binge drinking should be avoided. It seems wisest for pregnant women, especially teens, to give up alcohol altogether.

Smoking has been shown to stunt the growth of unborn babies. Some girls think that a smaller baby will make giving birth easier, but this simply isn't true. Also, underweight babies are at risk of breathing and other health problems. It's never too late to give up smoking, even if the pregnancy is well advanced. Every day without cigarettes reduces the likelihood that the mother will have a **miscarriage** or go into **labor** prematurely, and improves the baby's chances of being healthy. "When I got pregnant, I thought, 'If I can't give up smoking now, I never will.' But it was really hard. My boyfriend kept me going." (Rosie, 15).

Snorting, smoking, or injecting any drug during pregnancy can have very serious consequences. Babies born to cocaine-addicted mothers are irritable and jumpy, impossible to cuddle, and difficult to feed. Some are born addicted to the drug.

It's not even safe to take over-the-counter drugs without checking first with a doctor. The **thalidomide** tragedy of the 1960s has made everyone aware of the possible harmful effects of any drug on an unborn baby.

Exercise

Young women often use alcohol, tobacco, and street drugs to help them relax. There are all sorts of other ways of relaxing, however, which are far healthier—exercising, for example. It's perfectly safe to start a gentle exercise program during pregnancy as long as it isn't so vigorous that it causes sickness or exhaustion. Walking and swimming are especially good forms of exercise to get in shape for labor.

It's best to stop drinking alcohol altogether during pregnancy.

Pregnancy Care

In the United States, pregnancy care is provided by midwives, family doctors, and obstetricians (doctors specializing in pregnancy and childbirth). Many women receive some of their care from each of these professionals.

There are a number of routine checks that take place each time pregnant women go to the hospital or clinic.

- Their blood pressure is checked. This is very important because high blood pressure reduces the efficiency of the **placenta** and puts the baby at risk.
- Their urine is tested for sugar and protein. Some women develop **diabetes** during pregnancy and this means that they need to be cared for by a doctor who specializes in diabetes. Protein in the urine often goes with high blood pressure, and is a warning sign that there may be problems with the pregnancy.
- The distance from the top of the **womb** to the pubic hairline is measured.
- The baby is palpated, which means that the doctor or midwife feels the baby through the abdomen to check on his size and find out his position in the womb.

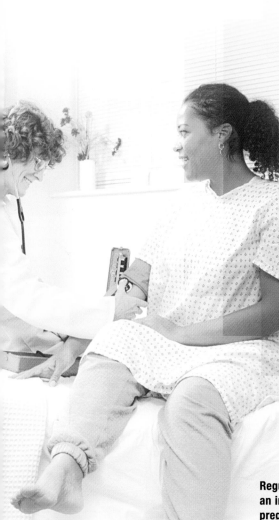

Regular check-ups are an important part of pregnancy.

Various blood tests are also carried out during pregnancy. These are to find out the woman's blood group, whether she is **Rhesus** positive or negative, whether she has **sickle-cell anemia** or **thalassemia,** and whether she is **anemic**.

At every clinic visit, the mother should be given the opportunity to discuss her worries in confidence. Health care professionals are trained to be non-judgmental. This is the time to talk about smoking, drug, or substance abuse and violent relationships as well as any other problems. Some young women might want to be checked for **sexually transmitted diseases** such as gonorrhea, which can cause premature **labor** if not treated. Specially trained nurses are available to offer **HIV** and AIDS counseling.

Many women take their partner or someone else with them to the hospital or clinic to keep them company and help them ask the questions they want answered.

❝❝I was frightened to ask questions in case I said something stupid. My social worker came with me and she found out the things I wanted to know.❞❞

(Lisa, 14)

As pregnancy goes on, the top of the bump gets higher and higher.

36 weeks ⟶

20 weeks ⟶

12 weeks ⟶

Is the baby healthy?

Women (and men) often have vivid dreams during pregnancy about their babies being abnormal in some way. It is natural to worry about whether the baby will be healthy. Some people are particularly worried about having a baby with disabilities such as Down's syndrome. Very young women are, in fact, at low risk of giving birth to a baby with Down's syndrome, but it does happen.

There are two kinds of tests that can be carried out during pregnancy to check the baby's health. **Screening tests** estimate the risk of the baby being abnormal. **Diagnostic tests** can say for certain whether the baby has a problem. Most women are offered a blood test to screen for **spina bifida** and Down syndrome between fifteen and eighteen weeks of pregnancy. A negative result means that the baby has only a very small chance of being abnormal. A positive result means that he has a higher chance. The results do not mean that the baby either definitely has or definitely doesn't have spina bifida or Down's syndrome.

Ultrasound scans can be screening or diagnostic. Sometimes, a scan shows quite clearly that there is a problem with the baby's spine, kidneys, or heart.

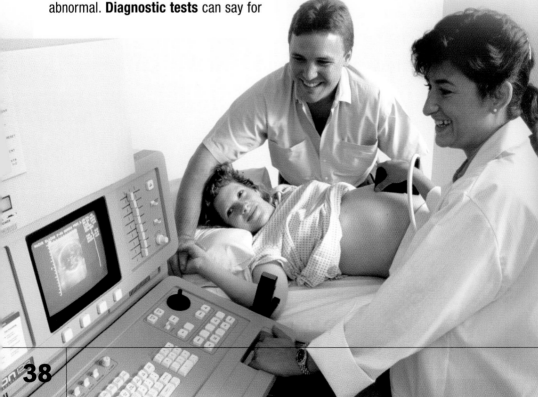

Other times, the scan is inconclusive. Chorionic villus sampling (CVS) and amniocentesis are diagnostic tests. When necessary, CVS is carried out at about eleven weeks of pregnancy and amniocentesis at eighteen weeks. The doctor puts a fine needle through the mother's abdomen and takes a small sample of either the **placenta** (CVS) or the **amniotic fluid** (amniocentesis). The medical laboratory analyzes the sample to find out whether the baby is healthy.

Both CVS and amniocentesis carry a 0.5 percent to 2 percent risk that the mother will miscarry following the procedure.

If a diagnostic test is positive, the mother has to decide whether she wants to continue with the pregnancy, or choose an **abortion.** Even if she wouldn't have an abortion under any circumstances, she might still want to have a test.

❝❝I would never have gotten rid of the baby. But I wanted the tests so that if she had something wrong with her, I'd be prepared.❞❞

(Becca, 17)

Giving Birth

Most girls are frightened about giving birth. They wonder how painful **labor** is going to be, and whether they will cope. Having someone to support them, such as their mother, best friend, or the baby's father, helps enormously.

Labor occurs in three stages. The first stage is when the **womb** starts to contract rhythmically and regularly, and the neck of the womb slowly opens until it is dilated 4 inches (10 centimeters). This usually takes from eight to eighteen hours. In the second stage of labor, the baby is pushed down the **vagina** by the powerful muscles of the womb and by the mother's pushing. This stage lasts from one to two hours. The **placenta** is delivered in the third stage of labor, which may last just a few minutes or a couple of hours.

Labor increases in intensity over a period of hours. When the contractions become very strong, most women find them painful. If left to their own devices, women will find many ways of helping themselves cope with the pain—changing their position, rocking their hips, rubbing their backs, and moaning. These are all natural forms of pain relief. There are also drugs available to help with pain. These may have unwanted side effects for both mother and baby.

It's important to have a special friend there for you in labor.

Giving permission

Giving birth in a hospital generally involves various medical procedures. These may be welcomed by the mother or they may leave her feeling out of control. It is important that she gives her permission before any procedure is carried out, and that she is kept fully informed about the progress of her labor and her baby's well-being.

When the baby is born, the mother and father, if he is present, need time together to bond as a new family. Parents enjoy stroking their baby, counting his fingers and toes, and holding him skin to skin. "Soon after she was born, we were left alone. Holding the baby was just amazing. Jon, my partner, cried. She was so beautiful." (Louisa, 19).

Is Breast Best?

A newborn baby needs to be fed milk. Breast milk is definitely best for babies, but breast-feeding may not always be best for mothers. Girls who dislike the idea of breast-feeding will be happier giving their baby bottles, and should not be made to feel guilty about their choice. The father's feelings are very influential. If he is supportive, breast-feeding is much more likely to be successful than if he is not. "Some of my friends made remarks about my girlfriend breast-feeding. But I didn't want my baby to have bottles. I think breast milk is the natural thing." (Noel, 18).

Breast-feeding has some advantages. Milk is always ready for the baby as soon as he or she is hungry. It comes at the right temperature and costs nothing. As the baby grows, the composition of the breast milk changes to match his or her needs. **Formula** is expensive and needs to be mixed and heated.

Breast milk is one option for feeding your baby.

Making a choice

Numerous medical organizations, including the American Academy of Pediatrics (AAP), are strong proponents of breast-feeding. "Human milk and infant formula are different," writes the AAP. "Not only does human milk provide all the protein, sugar, fat, and vitamins your baby needs to be healthy, but it has special benefits that formulas cannot match. It helps protect your baby against certain diseases and infections. Because of the protective substances in human milk, breastfed children are less likely to have ear infections (otitis media), allergies (such as **eczema** and **asthma**), diarrhea, pneumonia, wheezing, and meningitis."

Studies also indicate that breastfed babies are less likely to get **diabetes** and **multiple sclerosis.** Women who breast-feed are less likely to suffer from breast cancer and **osteoporosis.**

Many women prefer to breast-feed their babies, but it can be difficult to choose breast-feeding when you are attending school or work during the day. Babies that are being breastfed need to eat more often than babies that are fed bottled formula. Women who are working or at school may find bottle feeding more convenient, and it is just as healthy.

Some groups advertise to encourage mothers to breast-feed their babies.

Life with a baby

What is it like to be a teenage parent? Some teenage parents are married or in a stable relationship. It's more difficult for those who are not:

Nadia, 18:

"I split up with my boyfriend when I was five months pregnant. He definitely did not want to be a father. After the baby was born, I went back home to live with my mom. The house was small enough before, but with all the baby stuff, there was no room at all. I was tired for weeks on end. The baby kept waking up in the night, and he wanted attention all day. My mom was great, but she got tired too because she works full time. It took forever to get anything done. Taking a shower and getting dressed took me until the afternoon. Meeting friends was nice but I felt I didn't have much in common with them.

"After a while, things got easier. Jamie (my baby) started sleeping for longer and I was more organized. It was still hard to have a decent social life. I really missed my freedom. Jamie's three now and my youth worker has found a nursery school for him. I'm starting to think about my future. I want to take some classes and find a job so that Jamie and I can have a good life together."

Sharon, 17:

"My parents said I shouldn't see Mike anymore after I got pregnant. But we stuck together. He's twenty. He's working and we have a small apartment. We want to move to a place with a garden so that Ellie can play outside. She's nearly two now and she's gorgeous, but it's hard to find time for me and Mike with her around. I'm not sorry I had her, but I'd advise anyone my age to think very carefully about getting pregnant. If you want a baby, fine. But don't end up having one because you didn't bother to use a **condom.**"

Lucy, youth worker:

"To be honest, I'm amazed at how well some young women cope with having a baby. They've got virtually no money and they're living in these little run-down apartments, but they survive. They're really strong. But a lot of teenagers find being a parent too hard, especially if they don't have any support. The baby ends up in foster care. That's very sad; it's not good for the mothers and it's not good for the babies."

Babies and moms need to get out of the house.

Legal Matters

Age of consent

In the United States, the age at which young people can legally consent to have sex with someone of the opposite sex varies from state to state. In most states, the age of consent is 16 to 18 years old. Legally, an adult who has sexual relations with a minor can be charged with statutory rape.

Contraception

Many contraceptives (such as **condoms** and creams) can be purchased legally at any drugstore or supermarket. Currently, no federal laws (and only one state law) require a minor to obtain parental permission to get other contraceptive services. Since the 1970s, the trend has been toward allowing teenagers to make health care and **contraceptive** decisions for themselves.

Abortion

In the United States, 30 states currently require consent or notification of at least one parent before an **abortion** can be performed on a minor.

"Parental consent" means that a minor must get permission from a parent. "Parental notification" means that a minor must tell a parent, but doesn't need their permission.

It can be difficult to tell people, especially your parents, that you are going to have a baby. However, it is important to have someone you can confide in to help you through the process.

Adoption and foster care

In every U.S. state, both the birth mother and birth father (if the father has been legally recognized) must consent to giving up a child for adoption. The time frame for giving a child up for adoption varies from state to state. Many states require a waiting period (anywhere from 12 to 72 hours after the child's birth) before the birth parents can give the child up for adoption. In most states, a minor is treated no differently than an adult during the adoption process. In some cases, a child may be placed in temporary **foster care,** and the birth parents retain legal custody.

Avoiding Pregnancy

Taking responsibility for not getting pregnant means using some form of **contraception** or not having sex. Having fun with a boyfriend or girlfriend doesn't necessarily mean making love. Sometimes, sex can spoil a relationship rather than improve it. Young people who wait to have sex until they are in their late teens or early twenties are less at risk of **sexually transmitted diseases** and unwanted pregnancies. They enjoy sex more because they are more confident and more able to make up their own minds about what they want to do and what they don't.

In the United States, statistics show that one in four teenage mothers has a second child within two years of her first. For some, the pregnancy is planned, but often it's not. Some people think you can't get pregnant if you have sex in the bathtub, or if the girl has a shower immediately afterwards, or if she **douches** her **vagina** with vinegar. None of these are true.

It's possible for a girl to become pregnant after having a baby even before her **periods** start again. It's important to talk to a health professional about contraception before the baby is born.

Condoms

Condoms are the only form of contraception that offer protection against sexually transmitted diseases and prevent pregnancy (they are 98 percent effective). They're easy to buy and can often be obtained free from family planning clinics. Many experts recommend latex condoms used in conjunction with a spermicidal jelly. Using a **lubricant** on the condom also makes sex easier, but oil-based lubricants or creams may damage the condom and make it more likely to split. A **female condom** (95 percent protection against pregnancy) is also available.

Some girls think that carrying condoms around or going to a clinic to get contraception will make them look easy. Some boys think that having a condom in their pocket makes it look as if they are expecting to have sex. However, they are simply behaving responsibly.

Birth control pill

Widely popular, the birth control pill is made up of estrogen and progestin (female hormones). It requires a doctor's visit and prescription, and must be taken every day to be effective. The pill works by keeping a woman from ovulating (releasing an egg from her ovary each month). Since the pill does not stop the spread of sexually transmitted diseases, condoms should still be used. It is not safe to borrow pills from a sister or a friend.

Different contraceptives suit different people, but only condoms protect against pregnancy _and_ sexually transmitted diseases.

Injections and implants

Some girls find it very hard to remember to take the pill each day. For them, a **contraceptive** injection, or an **implant** placed under the skin of the upper arm, might be more suitable. An injection such as Depo-Provera lasts for twelve weeks and an implant is effective for up to three years. When the implant is taken out, the girl's normal level of **fertility** returns immediately. Again, neither of these forms of contraception are effective against sexually transmitted diseases, and should be used in conjunction with a **condom.**

IUS and IUD

An **intrauterine system** (IUS) or **device** (IUD) placed in the **womb** is effective for five years or longer, but can be taken out at any time. Neither of these methods are considered suitable for teens. Also, IUDs may increase the risk of **sexually transmitted diseases.**

Diaphragm or cap

A **diaphragm** (sometimes called a cap) is a choice for girls who want to use contraception only when they have sex. The diaphragm is put into the **vagina** a short time before **sexual intercourse** takes place. A doctor must fit you for a diaphragm. The diaphragm does not offer protection against sexually transmitted infections as a condom does.

Visit a doctor or health clinic to learn about using contraceptives.

Natural family planning

Some people have religious objections to contraception. They prefer natural family planning, which can be effective if properly used. Women have to be carefully trained to use this method of contraception, which involves examining the **mucus** in the vagina to see whether it is a safe time of the month to have sex. This form of contraception is the least reliable, and offers no protection against sexually transmitted diseases.

Talk to friends and, if possible, family members, about which contraceptives they use.

Emergency contraception

There are two methods of emergency contraception which can be used after having unprotected sex.

1. The so-called "Morning After" pill must be prescribed by a doctor. This method must be started within 72 hours of sexual intercourse; the earlier the better.

2. If fitted within five days of intercourse, an IUD can prevent a fertilized egg from implanting in the uterus.

In most states, you need to get a prescription from a licensed health care provider in order to get emergency contraceptive pills. Details on how to find contraceptive services are given on page 52.

Information and Advice

There are many organizations that provide confidential counseling and help for young people in crisis.

Advocates for Youth
www.advocatesforyouth.org
1025 Vermont Avenue NW, Suite 200
Washington, DC 20005
(202) 347-5700

Advocates for Youth is dedicated to creating programs and promoting policies which help young people make informed and responsible decisions about their sexual health. Advocates for Youth provides information, training, and advocacy to youth-serving organizations, policy makers, and the media in the U.S. and internationally. Their Web site includes information on HIV prevention, sexuality education, and teen pregnancy prevention.

America's Pregnancy Helpline
1425 Greenway Drive, Suite 440
Las Colinas, TX 75038
(888) 4-OPTIONS

This organization is committed to informing women in unplanned pregnancies of the many resources and services available to help them. It is their goal to provide each woman with a sense of empowerment and hope and to connect her with services in her geographical area.

Coalition for Positive Sexuality
P.O. Box 77212
Washington, DC 20013-7212
(773) 604-1654

The Coalition for Positive Sexuality provides straightforw information to facilitate discussions surrounding safe se birth control, pregnancy, and sexually transmitted diseas

Girls Incorporated
120 Wall Street
New York, NY 10005-3902
(800) 374-4475

For over 50 years, Girls Incorporated has dedicated itsel helping girls grow into strong, smart and bold young wo In addition to research and advocacy, Girls Incorporated conducts programs addressing pregnancy prevention, adolescent health, media literacy, substance abuse prevention, and sports participation.

The National Campaign To Prevent Teen Pregnancy
1776 Massachusetts Ave. NW, Suite 200
Washington, DC 20036.
(202) 478-8500

The National Campaign to Prevent Teen Pregnancy leads nation in drawing attention to the issue of teen pregnanc and providing technical assistance to state and local programs. The National Campaign's Web site contains f and statistics about teen pregnancy in the United States, for parents, and other helpful resources.

More Books to Read

Day, Nancy. *Abortion: Debating the Issue.* Berkeley Heights, NJ: Enslow Publishers, 1995.

Durrett, Deanne. *The Abortion Conflict: A Pro/Con Issue.* Berkeley Heights, NJ: Enslow Publishers, 2000.

Endersbe, Julie. *Sexual Readiness: When Is It Right?.* Mankato, Minn.: Capstone Press, 2000.

Endersbe, Julie. *Teen Fathers: Getting Involved.* Mankato, Minn.: Capstone Press, 2000.

Endersbe, Julie. *Teen Mothers: Raising a Baby.* Mankato, Minn.: Capstone Press, 2000.

Endersbe, Julie. *Teen Pregnancy: Tough Choices.* Mankato, Minn.: Capstone Press, 2000.

Endersbe, Julie. *Teen Sex: Risks and Consequences.* Mankato, Minn.: Capstone Press, 2000.

Hales, Dianne. *Pregnancy & Birth.* Broomall, Penn.: Chelsea House, 2000.

Lowenstein, Felicia. *The Abortion Battle: Looking at Both Sides.* Berkeley Heights, NJ: Enslow Publishers, 1996.

Peacock, Judith. *Birth Control and Protection: Options for Teens.* Mankato, Minn.: Capstone Press, 2000.

Peacock, Judith. *Dating and Sex: Defining and Setting Boundaries.* Mankato, Minn.: Capstone Press, 2000.

Winkler, Kathleen. *Teens and Pregnancy.* Berkeley Heights, NJ: Enslow Publishers, 2000.

Glossary

abortion
when doctors bring a pregnancy to an end using drugs or surgery

abusive relationship
when a girl's relative or partner forces her to have sex against her will, or hits, hurts, or humiliates her

amniotic fluid
water surrounding the baby in the womb

anemia
having too few red blood cells; causes tiredness, breathlessness, and loss of appetite

asthma
allergic disease that causes breathing difficulties

bladder
where urine collects until you go to the bathroom

cervix
neck of the womb which opens during labor so that the baby can be born

circulation
flow of blood in the body

condom
soft, rubber sheath placed over the penis to prevent pregnancy and protect against sexual infections

contraceptive
something that prevents pregnancy

diabetes
a metabolic disorder caused by improper sugar levels in the blood

diagnostic test
test that can identify a particular disease

diaphragm
rubber cap, shaped like a saucer, that fits inside the vagina over the opening of the womb

DNA
substance that carries genetic information in living cells

douche
flushing out the vagina with water or other substances

eczema
allergy which makes the skin red, sore, and itchy

female condom
soft, plastic pouch which lines the inside of the vagina to prevent the man's sperm from reaching the woman's womb during sex

fertility
ability of a woman to conceive a baby

fetus
unborn baby

formula
milk made from cow's milk and given to babies who are not breastfed

foster care
a system in which families temporarily care for a child or young person who is not their own

general anesthetic
drug to make patients unconscious during surgery

hormones
chemical messengers that cause changes in certain parts of the body, especially during pregnancy and labor

HIV
Human Immunodeficiency Virus; the virus that causes AIDS

implant
contraceptive placed under the woman's skin

intrauterine device (IUD)
small object put into the womb to prevent pregnancy

intrauterine system (IUS)
small object put into the womb that releases a chemical to prevent pregnancy

labor
process of giving birth to a baby

lanugo
fine hair covering an unborn baby from the fifth to eighth month of pregnancy

lubricant
any substance that prevents rubbing or friction

miscarriage
when a woman loses a baby during the first 28 weeks of pregnancy

mucus
sticky, jelly-like substance produced by the vagina to keep it moist

multiple sclerosis
disease affecting the nervous system

osteoporosis
disease affecting the bones of the back, pelvis, ribs, arms, and legs; common in older women

peer group
friends of equal standing most likely to influence someone's behavior

period
loss of blood from the vagina which women experience monthly from about the age of 12 until 50. Periods stop during pregnancy.

placenta
during pregnancy, the placenta (or afterbirth) passes food and oxygen from the mother to the baby; once the baby is born, the body pushes it out of the womb

premature baby
baby who is born before 37 weeks of pregnancy

Rhesus
people whose blood has the Rhesus Factor are *Rhesus positive*; people who don't have the Rhesus Factor are *Rhesus negative*

rubella
infection also called German Measles which causes abnormalities in the baby if the mother catches it during the first three months of pregnancy

screening test
test to separate people at low risk of a disease from those at higher risk and who need further tests

sexual intercourse
when the penis is inserted into the vagina

sexually transmitted disease
diseases such as syphilis, gonorrhea, and HIV often caught through having sex with someone who already has the infection

sickle cell anemia
disease caused by abnormally shaped red blood cells

spina bifida
condition where the baby's spine is not complete, often leading to paralysis

sterilization
using steam, chemicals, or very high temperatures to kill harmful bacteria

Sudden Infant Death Syndrome (SIDS)
also called crib death, the sudden and unexplained death of an apparently healthy baby

thalidomide
drug once given to treat morning sickness, later found to cause serious deformities in babies

toxoplasmosis
infection that can be caught from cat feces; if a pregnant woman becomes infected, her baby might have brain and eye abnormalities

trimester
pregnancy is divided into first, middle, and final trimesters, each lasting three months

ultrasound scan
use of sound technology so that the unborn baby can be seen on a visual monitor

vaccination
injections to protect against serious infections such as tetanus, diphtheria, and rubella

vagina
passage between a woman's legs which the penis enters during sex and which the baby comes down to be born

womb
sometimes called uterus; where the baby grows during the nine months of pregnancy

Index